Staggered Lights

Dennis Nurkse

Owl Creek Press
1620 N. 45th St.
Seattle WA 98103

ACKNOWLEDGMENTS

Grateful acknowledgment is made to the following publications in which some of these poems previously appeared.

The American Poetry Review
The California Quarterly
Columbia
Connecticut River Review
Green's Magazine (Canada)
Hanging Loose
Hoboken Terminal
Jeopardy
Lips
Little Balkans Review
Madrona
Montana Review
Mss.
New Letters
Pinchpenny
Pulpsmith
Southern Humanities Review
Stone Country
Telescope
This Is Important
Yellow Silk

This book was written with the support of a fellowship in poetry from the National Endowment for the Arts.

cover art by Wesley Wehr

contents copyright © Dennis Nurkse 1990

CONTENTS

SPEEDING

Lovers	8
Small Countries	9
The House on the Border	10
Grandmother's Exile	11
November Uprising	12
The Settlement	13
Ninety	14
The Operation	15
Time	16
Speeding	17
The Hole	18
Demobilization	19
Arrival in the Empire	20
K Street	21
Paradise	22
Travel by Night	23
Inside the Language	24
The Fire Door	25
The Dreaming Hand	26
The Year of Inflation	27

INROADS

Starting Again in the Orchard Country	30
The Windfall Mountains	31
Spring Breaking	32
Order	33
The Twin	34
The Engagement in the Plains	35
Formal Separation	36
Repairs	37
Emptiness	38
Walking on the Highway	39
Developing	40
Welding	41

Shyness	42
Work Glove	43
Signal Hills	44
The Old Religion	46
Talking in the Dark Bed	47
Barrier Islands	48
The Coast	49
Beginning with Evening	50

ON LEAVING THE EMPIRE

Winter Marriage	52
The Middle Game	53
Happiness	54
The Ladder	55
The Pact	56
Summer House	57
On Leaving the Empire	58
The Clearing in the Forest	59
Rented Houses	60
Closed Borders	61
Lamps and Fences	62

STAGGERED LIGHTS

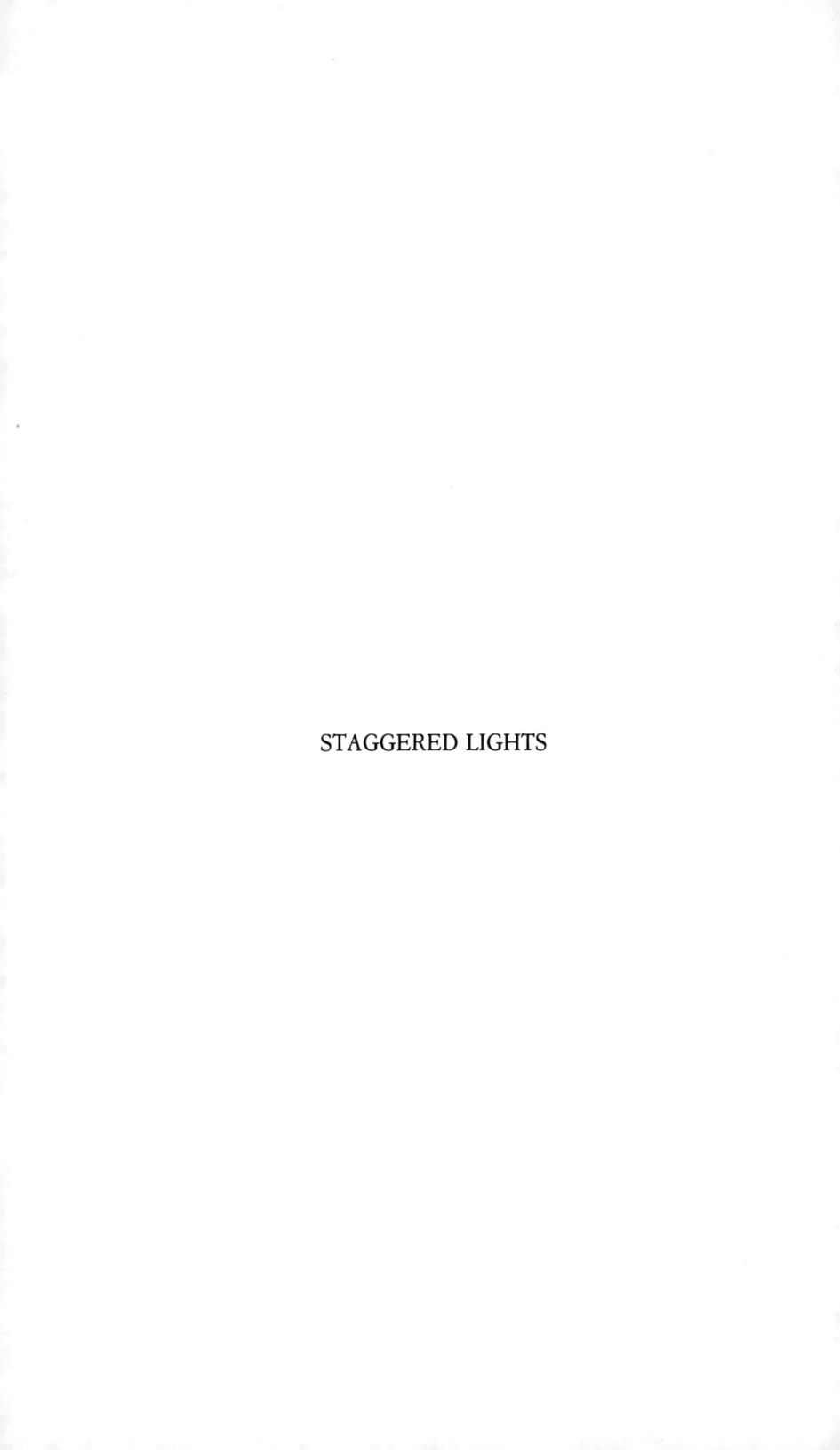

SPEEDING

LOVERS

We eat and sleep together,
share a narrow room.
If one has to wake suddenly,
the other lies in bed a moment
to finish both dreams.
Still we feel left over
from the deep past, pawns
from a shattered chessboard:
the grievance flaring between us
was settled long ago
without our knowledge, by armies
meeting in an unmapped swamp.
And always, steadier than rain on a roof,
we hear news of the weapon that can't be used.
We feel like children sent early to bed,
playing games with our enormous shadow,
making the image of the lion and the lamb
and then when the light is out turning inward
to run our fingers on the smooth cold wall.

SMALL COUNTRIES

A man and a woman
are lying together
listening to news of a war.
The radio dial
is the only light in the room.
Casualties are read out.
He thinks, "Those are people
I no longer have to love,"
and he touches her hair
and calls her name
but it sounds strange to her
like a stone left over
from a house already built.

THE HOUSE ON THE BORDER

Her lover is trapped
in the distant past.
I can hear his breath
and his heartbeat
when she makes herself still

and once she took me
to see the house he died in:
the floor ploughed by shells,
wires dangling, but the garden,
neatly maintained by neighbors,

culminates in blue foxglove
that will draw the butterflies
back from the forest.

GRANDMOTHER'S EXILE

The birds sang in a dead tree.
All summer, she'd heard the axe
in the pines, and branches collapsing
as if a bear were escaping
inland. At night all she heard
was the cistern leak,
until it froze in a string
and each drop was a pearl.
Then the wind came from Lapland.
She lost the hand to frostbite.
She called the ache in the phantom limb
"America," and when the sea calmed
she crossed it: the rest of her life
is accounted for, entered in code
in the blank front page of a King James Bible.

NOVEMBER UPRISING

My grandfather shaves in a cracked mirror
hung on a nail from the tallest oak.
Deeper in the forest, the Czar's soldiers
have ripped their lapels with vines.
They're waiting for the river to freeze.
That night, bridges will go up in smoke:
next day he'll wake in prison
surrounded by his sheep, and listen
as the bells toll twelve, and seven times seventy:
in the yard, a ring
of orphans prudently dancing.

THE SETTLEMENT

1945:   the batters
are swinging for the fences.
The wind drives all flies foul.
In a small town in Canada
my grandfather watches in disbelief:
he does not know
what the diagonal path
means for him, or what the wheat
stretching beyond the bleachers
to the Arctic means for his children.
In the ninth a ball lands fair:
the crowd shouts Ah; he whispers Ah.
At dusk a crystal radio
brings news of peace
in a Pacific Theater.
That night he dreams of the old country,
the wind bending the pines,
turning the lakes a color
blank as the name of God.
When he wakes he hunts
for that north wind and finds it
singing in the wire of his new enormous fence.

NINETY

I baked my grandmother
a cake with ninety candles.
She carried it across the icy road
to show to her girlfriend.
I trotted beside her, hoping
March wind would blow the flames out
and prove her age an illusion.
But she held the dish so steady
the tiny pillars of fire
supported nothing.

Her friend was ninety-five
and suggested: let the candles gutter
until the cake is covered with wax.
When the smells of fire and sweetness
were married, the black wine
was uncorked, and two cigars
shone in absolute darkness.

THE OPERATION

My grandmother says:
"I used the power of life.
Now I have other powers.
I don't want the doctors
ever to take off their masks.
Under my bed
I keep the key to the safe
and the jar of earth
from the old country,
remains of the time
when there was a keyhole
and an ocean:
before the pain came
when I separated it from terror
with my comb. Then I looked
in my compact and saw
lipstick on my grandmother's face."

TIME

In a dream I came to a city of porches
supported by wooden pillars, one sawn
a few inches off the ground.

I came to a street of shuttered houses:
some of the windows were *trompe-l'oeil*,
painted in perspective on limestone walls,
and one house was for sale.

I walked into a tearoom and there I met
my mother who has been dead three years.
Instantly I said, "I know you're really dead,"
and the trance remained between us like a glass partition
--we each came to one side and didn't try to break it,
afraid of being engulfed
in the wind from nowhere.

My brother had brought a companion,
an elderly lady, who complimented her
on the way her jacket matched her bag
and the way her hair was fixed, asking,
"How do you keep yourself
so pulled together?": my mother answered
instantly, a little bitterly
but also triumphantly, "Time."

And her friend, understanding
the will can use the pressure of days
to create form where there is none,
smiled and nodded and began
cutting a honeycake in ever smaller pieces.

SPEEDING

After death I inherited
and was rich enough at last
to get hurt for being understanding.

To be drunk one night means nothing,
but every night . . . and death is like that,
with its cunning and diplomacy.

I get too high. I wake
with cuts on my body like roads
to unknown territory.

I went to the bar at daybreak
and they were beating a man.
Was I hit that way last night?

My memory is vast and tender
with no face, no claim on you.

THE HOLE

It was early
when my father died:
May, a sun rising,
a clock about to strike.
The man who buried him
was a wrinkled peasant whose fathers
had dug the yard for centuries: he leaned
on his shovel cautiously, knowing
whose weight would make the grave.

He told me:
"Don't be ashamed
of your father's weakness."

DEMOBILIZATION

We staggered off the ship
and marched into bars,
looking for a fight.

But there were only old men
with yellow teeth, apologizing.

On a lit stage
girls in green eyeshades
played cards for no stakes.

ARRIVAL IN THE EMPIRE

Leaving her, I trotted
down the Fire steps. A hammer dangled,
chained to a glass door. From upstairs, a clarinet
played the A minor arpeggio so smoothly I couldn't tell
when the register changed. In the lobby
a carload of tourists from Florida
struggled with bags marked with labels
from prewar spas, telling the doorman,
"We'll catch you on the rebound," telling him,
"If you don't have problems, you're not alive":
and the doorman said nothing, but his eyes glittered
so I knew it was the same drug
that had quickened her heartbeat: I understood
my roots had gone deep enough
in the New World and knotted
around fear, and I won't be driven back:
no retreat to the old walled cities, where snow
was constant like unheard music, and the frontier
impassable as the line of sweat between two bodies
hugging on a rented bed.

K STREET

My lover lies naked
and the smoke fills the small room
like written language.
Then the wind blows it out.
In the numbness of deep need
we're edgy as garrison states.
We could destroy each other
again and again. For us, the weapons
are the strangers in the street
who shout for nickels in the rain.

PARADISE

One thread of paradise
is woven in her dress.
But only one. I turn over
the fabric while she's gone.
And I've lived all my life
learning how to endure pain,
how to sit in cheap hotels
and not ask, and be
empty like the bottle,
naked like the chair, narrow
like the crack in the thin cold wall.

TRAVEL BY NIGHT

At first our revolt
could only mimic
the power that held us captive
(so politely it seemed
a luxury to be afraid).

In your arms I felt
I had to give you a son
and give him money
and peace and rage
--give him them
in trust for you.

Other nights we were lost in each other
as if the door leading out had been smashed.

INSIDE THE LANGUAGE

I wish I could take care of myself
and not be fastened to you
and to the way I imagine you.

When we meet I'm glad I can't,
I'm glad you're unlike my hopes.
We rent a room above a neon sign
and the blue glare jumps in bed all night
casting shadows up. I never see the meaning
until I'm outside, late, looking back for you:
OCEAN HOTEL.

THE FIRE DOOR

We make love on the fire-escape
with the blank walls above
and the hard emptiness below
in the back of the city:
We remember to cry in, not out,
and rub together like falling leaves,
while on the other side of chintz curtains
your parents clatter, singing
rounds from the old country, already drunk
on the wine that was sealed for the wedding feast.

THE DREAMING HAND

I know thieves
better than I know myself.
I feel them smash my window
while a changing light
holds me a minute from home:
they'll take the document
I signed and forgot.

I lock my door
with many oiled keys
and sleep below the open window,
a razor in my dreaming hand.

THE YEAR OF INFLATION

Someone watches me
and crowbars my window
when I'm out.

Our loving keeps coming back
to a rifled room:
Who knows the other?

Like picking apart a daisy
saying: Accidental . . . Deliberate . . .

Everything is worth so little.
There is not one fragment
we can afford to surrender.

INROADS

STARTING AGAIN IN THE ORCHARD COUNTRY

"The new age is born,
the old rolls on unfinished."
The socks almost darned. The beams
trimmed, but as yet no roof.
In August heat we hate each other
and sleep together sopping.
A stranger comes at night
and stands in the garden
and sings in every unknown language.
In starlight his face is like my father's,
in lamplight like my mother's.
He opens his hands
to show he brought no weapon
though he comes from the land of sticks and stones.

THE WINDFALL MOUNTAINS

One orchard is separated from the next
by fences humming with faint current.
We pry slack wire open
with a fallen branch, squeeze through,
keep hiking toward the coast.
At twilight we find a shack
full of old ladders, and we make love
until we've lost all our credentials
in suffering, and we make love again
and give up all the authority
of being lost. Sometimes in the dark
we dream the cider company's hidden cameras
are recording us, but when we wake,
drifting blossoms have covered our trail.

SPRING BREAKING

The wind was in the house
with its grinding edge, its invisible
rope and scaffold, fine comb
and staggering clock: everything
except its perfect silence
that ploughed in a level field.
We tacked up canvas, swept, made love
in a trance of no-longer-waiting,
while wind blew in a streak
to Ontario without touching earth.
The city radio grew faint
and played less and less music.
I was scared I'd want to leave her
now the road was paved with jackpine,
the grade, shoulder and median strip
obliterated by mud from the river bottom.
I was scared of being the one
who stays behind, alone with a door
opening, opening, opening.
We had no fear of the wind
that pounded with a lover's weight
and left no seed.

ORDER

Last night I worked for an old artisan.
He sent me to his basement shop
with a weak flashlight, to mix concrete.
The tools and ruler on his pegboard
cast huge shadows, that did not
flinch when I snapped his droplights on:
only my body had no shadow.

Looking closer I saw
he was a maniac for order and had painted
the ideal forms of Hammer and Saw
in tar behind each appointed hook.

This is how I've lived
since I've known you: the tools
scatter, their shadows
stay put, to be polished,
to cut if necessary.

THE TWIN

A woman made a fool of me
night by night. She invited me
to concerts and didn't come:
I watched the violin bows glide
in a silence only I could hear
while drunks hummed along in waltz time.
She said she loved me,
then claimed she'd betrayed me
with a stranger invisible
as God or wind on a map.
But because of the wince I developed
and the look of defeat in my eyes,
her sister was awed and took me home
and confided childhood secrets,
her whisper moving backward
in time as her hands
wove shadow.

THE ENGAGEMENT IN THE PLAINS

Suddenly she didn't know me
the way the fencepost, the passing cars
and the silent owl don't know me:
This was some miracle of forgetting
forged in a narrow bed
in the empty part of summer
before dawn, when the clock stopped,
in the wheat country.

I looked up the words she'd spoken to me
and the pages had been ripped from the dictionary.
I poured over the album
showing her as a little girl
at play with her brothers and sisters
--her eyes had been erased.

Only a note taped to the mirror
invited me to meet her
in a bar in the market town
ruled by the evangelists.

I sat on my revolving stool
while dimpling churchwomen
in bridesmaids' gowns
passed into a dim back room.
Then I heard sighs, and glass shattering.

The goldfish in a tiny bowl
stared at me
as if astonished at my drunkenness:
staring back I understood
I'd grown old and my body
had become a trap:

Beyond it stretched the world of bitter work,
the stubble fields where the combine
gathers up the winter grain.

FORMAL SEPARATION

First I had to prove it really happened.
Because I was in love with her,
I would have lied about anything
just to hold her attention,
even if lying to the soul
is death.

Second I had to establish
it was me she meant to touch
in her deep absent way
when she lay down with her traveler
on the runway of the bankrupt airport.

Third I needed evidence: tapes and video
to be brought forward by a neutral party
--as if my memories could shift
like cargo, to the outside of my skull.

Last I require the miracle
that will allow me to understand
how she could go away
for a few hours each night, and nothing would change,
and time would still hold me
this tight . . .

Until it comes I keep packing to leave her
in the waiting room under the barred windows,
with the old men who spend all day arranging
a toothbrush, a torn glove, last year's magazines . . .

We buy no tickets
because we have too far to go.

REPAIRS

Waking, I see the tracks.

I drove here after midnight
past garages lit like gauge numbers
and a brickworks boarded up with plywood.
Behind the Traveler's Lodge I saw
a region of sky crisscrossed with wires,
the hook of a crane above a floodlit wall.

It's a repair yard
below my room,
a shunting-field.

A caboose from Duluth, blue chicory
pale with first light under the wheels.
A boxcar without doors
stuffed with black oranges.

I know each morning I wake here
the fog from the Ohio will lift a little,
I'll see more scattered hammers,
more ties, an older caboose.

At night I'll pretend I'm intimate
with what we were: a small shadow
tame under the lightswitch, a teacup
full of the local white wildflowers
called Nobody's Fault, the switch-signal
unflinching in chintz curtains.

In sleep my presentiment
will race ahead with a red fan-light,
while I trudge behind
and the steel parallels
converge on a fixed point
that exists only in memory.

EMPTINESS

All night I want you. Just to dream
beside you like a man on a treadmill
running in place. I wake before dawn and smoke
a menthol Tiparillo the previous tenant
left in my cupboard with a bottle of Roach-Prufe
and the spring to a flashlight. At lunch in the park
with you I feel nothing, I make puns, I break
French bread, a piece for you, for your lover,
crumbs for the birds. At dusk we go
to the district beyond the airport.
to see our lawyer. He folds his hands
and stares out the window. Among a million lights
one is brighter than ever before.

WALKING ON THE HIGHWAY

Curving shoulder
freeway above Burlington
lights of a minor city, and North
by Canada no lights. Good luck
is holy and bad luck the last town
with its rabbit coops and one boutique.
I've been traveling five years.
I still come to places seen in dreams
but not often. Lights of a saw mill
and a maple sugar shop. Almost dawn.
No traffic. Stars
high and oblique. By my fruits
I am known.

DEVELOPING

Sawdust and manmade altitude,
sun in profile on a hammer.
The crick in my neck
from framing the attic
is more fixed and durable
than the house itself.

God knows who'll live here.
We haven't finished grading the road
to the nearest small town, now obsolete
and prim and caught in childhood.

Landscapers are sending lawns
into the forest, like novice spies.
The pines' shiver is still a signal
to no-one in particular
but it carries only a measurable distance.

From the scaffold I can see the highway
though the bedrooms will face the trees.

A river of miniature flashing roofs and windows
saved by disappearance from being toys.

And there's already a hum
like a lawnmower running all Sunday,
and a hobbyist's sander whines at night,
voice of some implacable amateur.

WELDING

After the explosion
fatigue came like a broom
to sweep away the pieces.
A curtain was drawn and shrapnel
was teased from his throat.
A mask in many swift interventions
re-invented his hearing, as if building
a house out of burnt matchsticks.
Then he could follow the TV quiz:
the prize went to whoever
could stand the least pain.
He approved the man in the next bed,
who complained of dying
before Bell ran out of numbers.
Finally he felt a suave hate
for his father and mother, for the ex-wife,
for everyone he'd learned to love
so painstakingly, before the needle
began to swerve on the pressurized tank.

SHYNESS

I love you. Your neighbor
hauls out blue sheets. A cloud
reflected in your window
looks hard as concrete.

I sit in a parked truck
lighting Lucky after Lucky
from the one red disk.

At the end of your street
workers on platforms
are scraping a man's lips
from a floodlit billboard.

WORK GLOVE

I left a glove in your room
so I could come back. It had
a hole in the index. I felt
I was coming back from death,
riding back from DeKalb.
I pressed your bell repeating
under my breath: I made a mistake.

SIGNAL HILLS

We were driving a ridge road
with no ordinance number,
marked by the names of closest towns,
the sign changing as you passed the place:
"Hawthorne . . . Yule,"
"Yule . . . Ringoes."

When the valley turned white
and the fog began rising,
the villages were hardly there:
lamps, chickenwire, a steeple
--then just a shift in the signs.

After an hour of inches
I parked on the shoulder
away from the drop
and started walking up,
groping for a ridge pine.
But I did not surface.
I came to a padlocked door
leading into the mountain.
Entrance to a mine gallery.
Then the cloud seemed
heavier than my body.

I called to you, needing
your answer for a thread
in my maze of no corners.
But you sounded
directly above me
and neutral, like a radio voice
that rides on a frequency
into space without turning back.

So I had to measure
your voice by mine,
white with white, wet leaf
by wet rock. You called
"Here" and I called "Here".

*

This way I'll come
back to my footprints, back
to the amber idling-light.

You'll be smoking,
you won't want to talk.
In silence we'll come to Ringoes.
You will be silent in the empty tavern
until you step to the juke-box
humming the song you need to hear.

THE OLD RELIGION

Every night the tambourines
of the storefront church
downstairs, the guitar
resolving and resolving, the saved
chanting thanks
every night: and us
sometimes in love, sometimes
hating each other, sometimes
not even keeping track, just lying
watching the clouds
in the skylight, and listening
for something the drum's
always about to explain.

TALKING IN THE DARK BED

When we made love
our bodies were paradise
knowledge and freedom.

But afterwards we asked each other
do you believe in the war coming?
Do you believe in death?

If we said Yes
we were strangers
but if we said No
we were still strangers
hating each other for sleeping
with the bodies in the faceless crowd.

BARRIER ISLANDS

The tide passed over us.
Then we slept as before,
but tasting in each other furrows
and forests of distance deeply rooted.

We lived in hotels paid by the hour
after the end of vacation.
The windows glittered one by one
so long as there was writing
in Arabic, on the sea's face.

In the drawer and bed we found shells,
their spark of warning now disbelief,
whatever lived there had retreated
to an emptiness larger than the air.

THE COAST

My love is heavy
with the unborn child.
Since we've learned
to keep our mouths shut,
the old men talk to us
expecting no answers.
They show us the pails
of sea-bass and porgies
and fish too small to have names
rigged for bait. They let us
feel in our palms the cold sinkers
that will carry the line
against night and the oncoming tide.
They bend over salt-hard knots,
loving being known
as fishermen, not fathers.

BEGINNING WITH EVENING

I cradled my newborn daughter,
bloodflecked, blue, howling.
I felt empty as a suit
folded on a chair.
I sat in doctor's scrub
in a room where surgeons
were sewing up my lover's womb.
A nurse going off duty
commanded me: "Hold the face
away from the light
so the eyes can open"
and the eyes did open.

ON LEAVING THE EMPIRE

WINTER MARRIAGE

We've spent all our lives
together. Now the unknown
is beginning to come between us.
It's almost solid, like a curtain.
We can almost decipher
which of our gestures
wove it. She touches a cup,
the cup becomes unknown.
I sip her coffee:
The taste has nothing to do
with night and day. We begin
to want each other like people
you can see only once. We take
long walks in a forest
until fatigue comes
to soothe us, and memory
to prepare us:
so many prints in snow.

THE MIDDLE GAME

I played chess with a friend
for ten years in the park. Now
he's bitter at my marriage. He feels
I'm abandoning his opposition and moving
to the inside. I deny it.
I say "Nothing has changed"
and let him win. I ride home
by taxi because the subways
are on strike. I tip the driver
with married money. I tell my wife:
"I'm isolated." She surprises me,
saying she's isolated too.

Towards dawn I can't sleep.
I take down the board
and play against myself.
I try to move my pieces
to the inside. She talks
in her dream, but the language
is the old one, without words.
Snow falls
with no noise of falling. Tomorrow
I'll wake late and see her footsteps
and the dog's small tracks
going to the silver park.

HAPPINESS

All day in the house by the river
I tried to force
my child to be thankful.

A cobweb linked
the rod to the sinker.

I wanted her to smile
just once.

At last, while she slept,
I felt the same force
begin to pry me open.

THE LADDER

I'm on the top rung
nailing down a shingle
that flapped last night.
I hear thunder in the North
and see three tiny jets
swing behind the mountains.
I hear my child crying, and footsteps,
and my wife's voice singing
or commanding: Nothing can happen.

THE PACT

When the treaty is signed
it says: the armies rule.
They've divided the earth.
But when the treaty is not renewed
the blank margin is savage, and contains
all the daydreams that spin through our minds
as we lie naked in summer twilight
waiting for our child to wake, waiting
for the swing to creak, listening
as an unfelt breeze turns
all the pages of an unread book.

SUMMER HOUSE

I rowed across Sayre Lake,
smooth as watch-crystal.

Tethered in the deep part,
a milk-gallon buoy
tugged up and up and up.

On the far shore a chained dog
lunged at me almost sobbing.
The deep calm
behind the yelp
was an echo.

*

Then suddenly I could hear
all the sounds of my wife's house.

The child half-laughing,
half-crying, trying to speak
or speaking the unknown language.

A dress rustling. The creak
of the rocker on the porch.

Hiding my oars
I walked under the pines.

When the dark lay heavy as an arm
across my shoulder, I could still smell
the cut grass from the lawn.

ON LEAVING THE EMPIRE

You turn down from the freeway
into an unlit city
and for an hour you roll through a suburb
where lawnsprinklers fling an emptiness
that tastes of night and fruit and cinders,
then the neighborhood changes: coal-buckets
prop doors open, a crane is locked
behind a chain-link fence. You see

a knot of men in the glare from a barber's pole
finishing an argument about the war.
You brake to ask the time,
but instead of consulting watches,
they glance at scars on their wrists,
and you understand: these are returnees,
this is the town we grew up in.

      As you drive on
a zero clicks on the odometer,
the needle climbs over sixty,
but you feel so motionless
compared to the fading amber lights.

THE CLEARING IN THE FOREST

A dog stepped in my path
and challenged me. I froze
and shouted: Where's the owner?
In the distance, between the sky
and the mountain face, our echoes merged.
When I grew hoarse, I whispered:
Sit, and at once he crouched,
and his tail swept the forest floor,
but still he growled. It was noon
and the drone from the hidden beehives
was almost deafening, almost drowsy.
I was looking for the exact spot
where my father died. Viewing the body
on its slab, my mind had pictured
a clearing in the forest:
now following a brook upstream
all I'd found was a rudder
of ripples, and shadow-
branches bent like oars.

RENTED HOUSES

Long after my father dies
I dream I'm a child held tight
in strong arms. I wake
in a dark house and listen
as the rain tests
each shingle. Falling back
in a doze light
as morning rain, I dream of repairs,
then wake and make them.

CLOSED BORDERS

The State draws a line
between my death and my father's.

He fell and was buried,
the shovel forgot him,
I forgot him.

But I take my place
in a line of travelers,
each with a suitcase
containing a damp toothbrush
and spare clothes.

There's no more past
to claim us.
We're marching to the shelters.

On the way we keep asking
the fire for death, as if
the fire had one last secret.

LAMPS AND FENCES

When the dead came into power
at first we did not notice

the stars were a little brighter
there were more roaches
wherever we walked
we killed something

since it was involuntary
it happened as if in secret

in the bars the prices
were written in chalk

the musicians were too eager to finish
though they remained true
to the old rage

When we made love
our thoughts turned to the hunted

and those turned back
from the frontier

Though the frontier was only
the meaning of a sound
in a language that had mastered us.

Dennis Nurkse has published one previous collection of poems, *Shadow Wars* and has received a creative writing fellowship from the National Endowment for the Arts. His poems have appeared in many top literary journals including *American Poetry Review, California Quarterly, Mss., Montana Review, Southern Humanities Review, New Letters* and many more.